James F. Loughlin

St. Patrick, the Father of a Sacred Nation

A Lecture

James F. Loughlin

St. Patrick, the Father of a Sacred Nation
A Lecture

ISBN/EAN: 9783743326811

Manufactured in Europe, USA, Canada, Australia, Japa

Cover: Foto ©ninafisch / pixelio.de

Manufactured and distributed by brebook publishing software
(www.brebook.com)

James F. Loughlin

St. Patrick, the Father of a Sacred Nation

PHILADELPHIA

ST. PATRICK,

THE FATHER OF A SACRED NATION.

"And the Lord said to Abram: 'Go forth out of thy
country, and from thy kindred, and out of thy
father's house; and come into the land which I
shall show thee. And I will make thee a great
nation, and I will bless thee and magnify thy
name, and thou shalt be blessed. I will bless
them that bless thee, and curse them that curse
thee; and in thee shall all the kindred of the
earth be blessed."—GENESIS XII.

ADDRESSING myself this even-
ing to the task, so dear to every
priest whose veins are warm
with Celtic blood, of paying this annual
tribute of praise to St. Patrick and the
consecrated land of our fathers, I must,
first of all, cast aside the vain hope of being
able to say anything new upon a subject
which for many generations has engaged
the talents of one of the most eloquent

(5)

races of the modern world. Fortunately,
you do not expect or wish to hear anything
new on this subject; the perennial charm
of the theme, like that of the old, familiar
melodies of our fatherland, lies mainly in
the hallowed memories which sway your
souls as you listen. I have, therefore, de-
termined to follow the well-beaten track;
and I have chosen for my text that passage
of Holy Writ which the wisdom of my
predecessors has oftenest selected as the
most appropriate. Indeed, there exists so
striking a resemblance between the office
and mission of the Irish apostle and his
children in the New Dispensation, and the
office and mission of the illustrious patriarch and his seed in the old, that this com-
mand given by Almighty God to Abraham,
and these promises made to him and his
descendants, may, without the change of
one iota, be transferred to St. Patrick and
his people. At a time when ignorance and

error were creeping over the earth and involving all the children of Adam in gross darkness, the Lord called Abraham forth from his country and his kindred to make him the father of a sacred nation, of a nation which should remain the dwelling-place of light and truth amidst the universal gloom, and which, in God's appointed time, should communicate its inherited blessings to all the kindred of the earth.

Now, coming down to the fifth century of the Christian era, we find in the calling of St. Patrick an exact counterpart to the calling of Abraham. True religion appeared to be once more upon the point of disappearing from the earth. The Eastern Churches, torn and debased by endless heresies, dissensions and schisms, were rapidly sinking into that miserable abyss of apostasy from which they have never since permanently arisen. The condition of the Western Church was equally critical;

for although, thanks to the transcendent genius of St. Augustine and the divine zeal and authority of the Roman Pontiffs, the pestilential tide of Pelagianism had been forced back to its native Britain, yet storm-clouds were gathering in the depths of the Northern forests and on the Eastern table-lands, which seemed fated to sweep away civilization, law, science and religion from the face of the globe. Already the first tremendous billows of barbarian invasion had rolled over Europe and spent their fury among the sands of Africa. Alaric the Goth had ravaged Italy and sacked Rome; Genseric the Vandal sat enthroned in the ancient city of Carthage. And this was but the beginning of evils; for innumerable hordes were still to come, urged on by love of adventure and lust of conquest, but yet more by their eagerness to escape the advancing shadow of the terrible Huns, those most savage of all barbarians, whose gigan-

tic empire, dreaded alike by Goth and Roman, was stretching itself over hills and
valleys, dense forests and lofty mountain
peaks, morasses, seas, rivers and trackless
deserts, from the wall of China to the banks
of the Rhine.

It was at this emergency that God spoke
to the heart of the great saint whose memory we are gathered to honor: " Go forth
out of thy country and from thy kindred
and out of thy father's house, and come
into the land which I shall show thee."
And where is this land which the Lord has
chosen ? Where is the home of those who
are to enjoy light whilst darkness enshrouds
the earth, and liberty whilst all Europe is
trampled under the feet of Goths and Huns
and Vandals ? Far away in the West there
stood an island, moderate in extent, wonderful in fertility, vying with the emerald in
beauty, whose rugged cliffs, beetling over
the unconquered ocean, marked the extreme

limit of the known world. This happy
island had been for untold centuries inhab-
ited by a people who, protected by their
watery ramparts from Scythian incursions
and Roman conquests, and unimbued with
the vain subtleties of Grecian philosophy,
maintained a sturdy independence, and
tenaciously adhered to the laws, the institutions and the religion of their ancestors.

So far as the natural character is concerned, the Irishman from his very first
appearance on the stage of history has pre-
served, almost unaltered, his well-known
characteristic traits. He has ever been
generous in his impulses, quick-witted, im-
pressionable and hospitable. The spirit
which pervaded the legislation of our
primitive ancestors was rather that of
modern than of ancient civilization. Three
things the Irish people have consistently
detested down from the days of Milesius—
despotism, the so-called "right of primo-

geniture" and landlordism — three evils,
whose baneful dominion in the island has
been founded on the ruins of the nation's
independence. By their ancient law of tanistry, all dignitaries in the land, from the
chief monarch down to the humblest can-
finny, were chosen by the free suffrages of
their countrymen. "The law of tanistry,"
says an unfriendly English historian (Lingard II, 86), "regulated the succession of
all dignities from the highest to the lowest.
It carefully excluded the sons from inheriting, as of right, the authority of their father;
and the tanist, or heir-apparent, was elected
by the suffrages of the sept during the
lifetime of the ruling chieftain. The eldest
of the name and family had, indeed, the
best title to this distinction; but his capa-
city and deserts were previously submitted
to examination, and the charge of crime, or
cowardice or deformity might be urged as
an insuperable objection to his appoint-

ment." So jealous were our forefathers of
their political liberties! Nor did it agree
with their notions of equity that the first-
born son should enjoy an exclusive or pre-
ponderating right of inheriting his father's
wealth. Their law of gavelkind prescribed
that a man's movable property should de-
scend to all his son's equally, without any
consideration to primogeniture. And what
about the land? Why, a landlord has always been an odious character in Ireland.
The primitive Irish preferred pasturage to
agriculture, and I believe that preference is
again become quite fashionable among the
landlords over there. A man in the olden
times possessed his land only so long as no
death occurred in his sept. But, to quote
Lingard, "at the death of each possessor
the landed property of the sept was thrown
into one common mass; a new division was
made by the equity or caprice of the can-
finny, and their respective portions were

assigned to the different heads of families
in the order of seniority." This regulation,
whilst it impresses us favorably as evincing
the national love of fair play, must still be
admitted to have been a crude and primitive arrangement. But it is amusing to observe that what modern socialists vaunt as
a novel invention of the nineteenth century
was fairly tried and wisely discarded centuries ago by the common sense of the Irish
people. Their criminal code bore the impress
of the national gentleness ; for it is agreed
that they always shrank from the actual in-
fliction of capital punishment. Their religion
consisted in the worship of all those great
objects in nature which are most apt to
excite the veneration of a race highly im-
aginative and poetical—the sun and moon,
the consuming flame and the running stream,
the mighty tempest, the awful mountain, ·
and, above all, the mysterious shade of
their oaken groves. And thus they con-

tinued for ages unmolested to sing to their
wild harps the praises of their gods and
the renown of their ancient heroes.

This is the nation which the Lord has
chosen for His peculiar inheritance; this
the land upon whose fair horizon the Sun
of Justice is about to rise, never more to
set. Ireland, hitherto thou hast borne no
yoke. Thy hills have never echoed the
shouts of invading legions; no captive
Irish Chieftain has ever graced the triumph
of a Roman General. But that which
Cæsar could not do, Christ will do. Pagan
Rome dared not attack thee; but Christian
Rome has already given the signal for the
assault. Behold, hastening over mountain
and sea, armed with a staff received from
JESUS, strengthened with ample jurisdiction
from the Supreme Pontiff, fearless, un-
daunted, Patrick advances, a host in himself. No novice in the apostolic warfare
is this new champion of Christianity. In-

ured to toil, as well by the hardships of
bondage as by long years of extraordinary
penances, instructed in the science of God
by the most distinguished masters of his
age, having served under two great com-
manders in a brilliant campaign against
heresy in Britain, he brings to the task
allotted him by Providence ability, skill,
experience and the prestige of past success.
He lands upon the coast of Erin, uplifts the
standard of the Cross and takes possession
of the island in the name of Christ and of
His Vicar. The peaceful glories of his
conquest it is needless to recount, for they
are indelibly engraven upon the hearts of
a grateful race. The Christian world
viewed with astonishment the unprece-
dented spectacle of a nation gained to the
faith without bloodshed, without persecu-
tion, almost without resistance. Never did
the arrows of the Divine word fly with
such swift and telling effect as when shot

from the lips of St. Patrick. That Gospel
which had fallen powerless upon the proud
ears of Epicureans and Stoics in the Areo-
pagus, although preached with all the in-
spired energy of St. Paul, fell with a crushing
weight upon the artless idolatry of Tara.
Before the triumphant march of the Irish
apostle idols fall and vanish forever; war-
like chieftains bow their heads to baptism;
princely youths and maidens put on the
monastic garb; the Druids are changed into
priests and bishops, and every harp within
the land is attuned to sing that Patrick's
God is become the God of Erin. Thus has
the obedience of the new patriarch, the
Christian Abraham, been amply rewarded.
He is in possession of the land which the
Lord had shown him. He is become the
father of a great nation, which, to the end
of time, will enshrine his blessed name in
their heart of hearts with religious enthusi-
asm. Generations shall come and go, but

the memory of St. Patrick will never fade.
Happy Ireland! which welcomed so great
an apostle; and happy apostle! whose lot
was cast among so affectionate a people.
But now his work is done, and the time
has arrived when the saint is destined to
receive a second call from Almighty God—
a call, this time, not to labor, but to repose,
not to go forth again upon a lifelong pil-
grimage, but to enter into his eternal home.
From his episcopal throne in Armagh the
aged conqueror beholds the entire nation
subject to his spiritual authority, and
through him subject to Rome, and through
Rome subject to Christ. Religion flour-
ishes throughout the land with the sim-
plicity of infancy combined with the full
vigor of manhood. How changed is Erin
now from what she was that day when
Patrick in his early youth was cast upon
her shore a despised and downcast slave.
And oh! if we were worthy, my friends,

2

to enter into the sanctuary of our venerable father's meditations, as he recalls one by one the events of his long and checkered career. It is only now, when the drama of his life is hastening to its close, that he can fully appreciate the beautiful unity of design which has reigned throughout it, and can perceive how all the occurrences of his life, even the most painful and the most mysterious, were by the hand of God woven skillfully into the great mission for which he had been chosen. But thy trials are now past, thy day's work is finished; "go forth," faithful servant of the Lord; thy Master's arms are extended to embrace thee.

In this supreme moment, one thought only, I think, disturbed the fullness of the saint's blessedness—the thought that in Ireland no one had been found in all these years of his labors who would add to his apostleship the crown of martyrdom. How

he envied St. Peter his cross, St. Paul his
sword, St. Bartholomew his knife, St. John
his caldron! He had been like these
princes of the Church in life, wherefore
shall he be unlike them in death? *They*
witnessed unto Christ amidst excruciating
torments; is he placidly to expire on his
couch? They died hooted and scoffed at
by an unbelieving populace; he finds himself surrounded by loving and attentive
children. What means this innovation
upon the fate of Apostles? But courage,
great saint; God looks not upon the gift,
but upon the heart. Though the Irish
are not a people destined to make martyrs,
but rather to become martyrs, yet has not
thy whole life been one prolonged martyrdom? Thy slavery, sanctified by prayer
and patience, was a martyrdom; thy sacri-
fice of country, of kindred and of the com-
forts of thy patrician home was a martyrdom; the ardent zeal which consumed thy

life in the hardships of the apostolate was a
martyrdom; and whatever may be wanting
to thy crown in the shape of torments or
persecutions thou shalt receive vicariously
in the heroic sufferings of thy children in
future ages. Happy fate! Ireland's apostle
suffers not *from* his children, but *in* them
and *with* them. I love to dwell upon this
sweet scene of St. Patrick's dying moments.
It is a spectacle of which Ireland alone can
boast. She alone manifested for her apostle
during his lifetime the same filial reverence
which she has paid to his memory since his
death. The nation stood at his bedside to
cheer his declining strength with tender
solicitude. And the saint, whose love for
his children was stronger than death, for-
getful of himself, concentrates his failing
energies upon the one great object of his
affections and his triumphs. Gather about
your aged father, children of Ireland, and
catch the last precious words which are

quivering upon his lips. "Grant me this favor, O Lord," he murmurs, "that my people may remain ever true to the faith I have taught them." With this prophetic prayer on his lips, the blessed man of God passed away to his heavenly home. He passed away; but his spirit remained with his people, and throughout all the vicissitudes of their extraordinary history they have remained ever "true to the faith."

Indeed, the history of Catholic Ireland seems to be only the sequel or prolongation of the life of her apostle, and, on the other hand, the life of St. Patrick might pass for an excellent allegory of the subsequent history of his people. That same admirable unity of design which we observe running through the life of St. Patrick, that same Providential shaping of all circumstances to the working out of a Divinely appointed mission, is unmistakably discernible in the history of Ireland. She was destined to be the sacred island, the eternal home of orthodoxy, the seminary of apostles; and this peculiar mission demanded and procured for her the special fostering care of Divine Providence. But, before advancing further, it may be useful to make a few preliminary remarks.

Man is a very complex piece of work, and may therefore be viewed from a hundred different standpoints. Hence the histories that can be written of him are as multifarious as are the relations in which he stands to things seen and unseen. Let the warrior, the statesman, the political economist, the scientist, the man of letters and the moralist, sit down to write histories of the self-same race or nation, and you will be surprised at the kaleidoscopic variety of their respective productions. The man of war will entertain you with a narration of brilliant exploits on field and wave. Kings and emperors at the head of mighty armaments are his heroes; sieges and battles, the impetuous charge and the gallant repulse, the roar of the cannon and the gleam of the bayonet—these form the matter of his drama. The statesman leads you into the cabinet of princes, to teach you how treaties are concluded, laws enacted and the populace ruled. The political economist revels among bewildering statistics, shows how the resources of a country are developed, and expounds the philosophy of supply and demand. The scientist follows the student into his quiet chamber, and traces the steady advancement of human knowledge. The man of letters narrates the growth of literature and language. The moralist studies the vicissitudes of the eternal struggle between virtue and vice. Humanity presents a different aspect to each of these historians; and very often an age which is pronounced by one of them most dismal and disastrous will be lauded by another as the brightest in the annals of the race. I have mentioned several classes of historians; but these do not exhaust the capabilities of the subject. There is another relation in which a man or a nation may be viewed; and it is the highest and noblest of all our relations —our relation toward our Almighty Creator. This is not only our highest relation; it is, moreover, one which animates all the other relations. Men were not created to be food for cannon, as the warrior seems to suppose; nor to be the dupes of politicians; nor for any other terrestrial object, high or low. Man's destiny is to work out the supreme designs of Divine Providence. That historian is, therefore, the wisest who, with due reverence, endeavors to read human events in the light of God's high decrees.

Now, Ireland's destiny is so patent that he who runs may read it. Geographically secluded from the profane world, she was

chosen by the Almighty, like Palestine of
old, to be His inalienable inheritance, the
impregnable citadel of Revelation and the
seminary of an Apostolic race. In a world
so tempestuous as this, where decay and
mortality are written upon the face of all
things, where the greatest nations, as well
as individuals, are prone to fall and to become persecutors of that faith of which
they are the natural protectors, it was necessary that the Church should have some
nation upon whose fidelity she could se-
curely rely, and from whose bosom she
could, in times of dire distress, replenish
her spent forces. That chosen nation is
Ireland, my friends. Whilst Rome has
always been, and will always remain, the
head of the Church, Ireland is her right
arm. The Roman Pontiff is the General-
in-Chief of the people of God; but the
Irish are his forlorn hope, ever to be found
in the thickest of the combat, passionately

attached to their Chieftain, and yielding a filial and rational obedience to his venerable commands. In thus extolling Ireland I have no wish to rob other nations of their . due meed of praise. Many of them have deserved well of the faith. Many of them have powerfully contributed to its propagation and suffered much for its preservation. But none of them contests with our Isle of the Saints the honor of being in the most complete and tender manner consecrated to the religion of Jesus Christ. All other nations have a profane as well as a sacred history. They have achieved power and glory through wars waged in other interests than those of religion—interests oftentimes opposed to those of religion. The history of Ireland since her conversion, on the contrary, has become thoroughly identified with that of her religion. Her national greatness and her national glory are derived from her faith. If she has taken to arms, it has been to defend her faith; for Ireland's enemies have invariably begun by overturning her altars.

I am aware that this supernatural way of presenting Irish history is not palatable to some individuals of our race who are tainted with the materialistic infidelity which infects the present age. *Some* there are—not many, indeed, for materialism and infidelity are snakes that do not thrive in Irish soil—who hear this Catholic doctrine with ill will. They think it likely to breed a fatalistic apathy in the national breast. They fear it may dull the edge of patriotism and reconcile the popular heart to oppression and treason. Impious folly! Do they imagine the Irish are like the Turks, that they cannot distinguish God's eternal purpose from man's petty malice? Believing as we do that Christ's sufferings were pre-

destined, are we the less disposed to de-
test the cowardice of the unjust judge,
the fury of the infatuated populace or the
base treachery of Judas Iscariot? You
forget, too, my infidel philosopher, that
we are discoursing, not upon Ireland's
unknown future, but upon her glorious
career in the past. That past cannot be
understood without a constant reference
to God's adorable counsels. To the eye
of the infidel history presents nothing but
a disjointed succession of contradictory
events, which follow each other without
order, without meaning. It is only when
we survey the life of an individual or of
a nation from the standpoint of Divine
Providence that we are enabled to soar
above " the whips and scorns of time, the
oppressor's wrong, the proud man's con-
tumely," and to seize things with the in-
telligent eye of the Christian philosopher.

But to return from this digression.

There are, as I remarked, so many points of analogy between the life of St. Patrick and the history of Catholic Ireland that a poetical mind might fancy the saint ended his mortal career only to begin life over again, on a grander scale, in his children. The life of St. Patrick divides itself into three distinct periods, the first two of which are preparatory to the glorious labors of the third. The first sixteen years of his life were years of peace and happiness, unmarred by sin or sorrow. During this period the young saint, sheltered from this evil world in the bosom of a religious home, and surrounded by models of Christian virtue, expanded in the rich bloom of unsullied innocence. Then followed the epoch of his trials in bondage, when the tender plant was plucked from its native soil and cast upon the bleak Northern hills. Here in the stern school of adversity the delicate became rugged; the child was developed into the man; and the modest youth began to dream of bold enterprises and vast spiritual conquests. Thus St. Patrick was trained to the Apostolate; and did not Divine Providence pursue the self-same course with the Irish nation? In the history of Catholic Ireland we discern these same distinct periods—the blameless childhood, the stormy adolescence and the apostolic manhood.

1. Whilst darkness and desolation were covering the rest of the earth—whilst Huns and Saxons, Goths and Vandals, Moors and Saracens were carrying despair and death into all corners of Europe, Asia and Africa—whilst one by one the bright lights of ancient Christendom—Jerusalem, Antioch, Alexandria, Carthage—were being extinguished—Ireland, exempted by a special grace of the Almighty from the universal misery, continued for three centuries to be the unmolested sanctuary of the

faith, the asylum of learning, the nursery of saints and missionaries. How wistfully we now look back through all the intervening horrors upon those happy days of the nation's childhood, when, quite unconscious of the dark future in store for her, she consecrated her virgin heart to the service of God; when churches and monasteries crowned each hill and nestled in each dale; when the air was ever laden with melodious psalmody and the perfume of prayer; when, unable to contain within her generous Celtic breast the fullness of her joy, she sent forth, as a presage of her future apostolic labors, her Columbas to the Isles of the North, her Columbanuses into the heart of Europe, and launched her Brandans upon the western waves to search out new realms for Christ.

The exceptional character of Ireland's position was fully appreciated by the other nations of Europe. She was looked upon

as sacred ground, and her people were
recognized as enjoying in a very special
manner the friendship of our Saviour. I
narrate a thrice-told tale. To her shelter-
ing bosom there flocked from all Christendom studious souls thirsty for knowledge,
repentant souls longing for seclusion, vir-
tuous souls in quest of refuge and models;
and they found knowledge in her schools,
discipline in her cloisters, and the humblest
peasants in the land could teach them, by
precept and example, the path of Christian
perfection. For the Irish at their conversion did not put on religion as an outward
garment. The Catholic faith sank deep
into their souls, and became the center of
their private and public life. It absorbed
and assimilated all their thoughts and aspirations. For their faith they lived and
studied; in it they reposed their individual
happiness and their national glory.

2. But a change was to come over the

face of the island. Indeed, these centuries
of happy tranquillity were intended to be
only a period of preparation, only an intro-
duction to its history. A Christian nation
can no more than a Christian individual
hope to follow Christ by any other way
than that of the Cross; and as well the
nation as the individual must employ such
periods of peace and quiet in preparation
for the struggle which is certain, sooner or
later, to supervene. That fateful day at
length arrived for Ireland. I can fancy,
my brethren, a scene in heaven like unto
that which ushered in the sorrows of pa-
tient Job. Once more, methinks, "on a
certain day when the sons of God came to
stand before the Lord," the foul prince of
darkness obtruded his hateful presence
upon that blessed company. Then spoke
our Divine Lord: "Hast thou considered
my chosen people, that there are none like
them in the earth, simple and upright men,

3

and fearing God and avoiding evil?" But
Satan, answering, said: "Doth Erin fear
God in vain? Hast not thou made a fence
for her and her house and all her substance
round about, blessed the works of her
hand, and her possession hath increased
on the earth? But stretch forth thy hand,
and touch all that she hath, and her bone
and her flesh, and then shalt thou see that
she will bless thee to Thy face." The Almighty, willing to glorify His elect and
the power of His grace, took up the chal-
lenge so impudently cast before Him, and
gave permission to Satan to wreak his fury
on the devoted nation, making, however,
the same reservation in her favor which He
had made in the case of His servant Job,
that the Evil One must spare its life. A
conflict thereupon ensued which stands
unparalleled in the annals of the human race.
Never were the engines of infernal warfare
brought to bear upon the children of men

with such preternatural skill, with such overwhelming force, with such fiendish cunning, with such stubborn persistence, yet never did the infernal serpent sustain so thorough, so crushing a defeat. Wars and famines; invasions, conquests, confiscations; the cruel steel of a ferocious soldiery; the brutal whip of an implanted band of robbers; the haughty insolence of a State-fed heretical clergy, and the canting hypocrisy of swarms of professional proselytizers; the ingenious machinery of an infamous legislation—in fact, what evils that can afflict a nation were not made use of in the attempt to eradicate the faith from the breasts of the Irish? Yet every new onslaught of the enemy issued in a fresh triumph for Catholic Ireland. Satan wrested from her everything but that which was the sole aim of all his efforts— her Faith.

No doubt, my friends, the subject of Ire-

land's unutterable woes has often forced itself upon your minds, and at the remem-
brance of her sufferings the tear has sprung
to your eye, and your cheeks have burned
and your breast heaved with just indigna-
tion at the inhuman wretches who, age
after age, have lent themselves to Satan to
be the instruments of his cruelty. But
have you never looked beyond the physical
miseries of each day and hour? Or have
the wails of Erin's exiles, the dying moans
of her outcast children, as they famish by
the wayside, and the bitter torments of her
legions of martyrs so stunned your soul as
to make you incapable of appreciating the
moral grandeur of the scene? Oh, then,
you have never conceived thoughts worthy
of Ireland! You have seen nothing but
her humiliations; you have not discovered
the Divine glory which shines through
them. You have seen the wretched work
of man, but not the all-shaping, merciful

hand of God. My mission, brethren, is one, not of hatred, but of charity; hence you must not expect to hear from me either a pathetic narration of Ireland's wrongs or a vehement invective against her oppressors. Indeed, whilst I am very far from wishing to extenuate the infamy of those who have outraged and devastated the land of our fathers, yet, instead of fostering rancor against them, I feel more disposed to bless their infatuated malice, which, under the supreme control of Providence, has so chastened and sanctified the nation as to make it the model of Christendom. If Ireland, like the other nations, had " rested on her lees, and had not been poured from vessel to vessel nor gone into captivity" (Jer. 48: 11), she, too, would have been a profane nation, with her measure of worldly greatness and with worldly ambitions and aspirations; but she would not have attained that noble station in the

Church to which she was predestined, and
for which a long series of trials was the
indispensable preparation.   Who does not
sympathize with St. Patrick under the lash
of his captors?   But Patrick's bondage was
necessary for Ireland; and, brethren, Ireland's bondage was necessary for the world.
She was led into captivity, not only that
the world might have a brilliant illustration
of the heroism of Christian patience and
resignation, but, especially, that it might
have what it sorely needed, a nation of
Apostles.

3. Yes, my friends, after withstanding for
ages the open violence and the insidious
wiles of Satan, Ireland was advanced to
the highest station in the Church.   "God,"
says St. Paul, "has placed in His Church,
first of all, the Apostles;" and by an unparalleled grace the Irish people were raised
in mass to this sublime office.   Other nations have, indeed, given birth to illustrious

apostles. Spain may well be proud of St. Francis Xavier, Britain of St. Boniface and Italy of St. Augustine. But Ireland has done still more: she has not sent forth isolated missionaries; she has gone forth herself to the extreme ends of the earth. Oh, how often in these latter days has not that stern but salutary voice of God resounded through the island: " Go forth out of thy country and from thy kindred and out of thy father's house;" and even though that high decree came disguised in the harsh tones of a bailiff, with what filial acquiescence in the Divine Will have not millions of her children bidden a sad farewell to their native land, their humble hearth and their dearest kindred, and gone forth to penetrate the wilds of America, the jungles of India and the sands of Australia! Truly, " there are no speeches nor languages where their voices are not heard; their sound is gone forth into all the earth."

With unflagging zeal and superhuman endurance they have planted the faith under every star of heaven, making the desert and the wilderness bloom with all the beauty of Carmel and Saron. Oh! island of the saints, how sublime is thy destiny! Everything pertaining to thee is extraordinary and supernatural. Thou seemest to belong to a different world from this, thou art so unlike the other nations of the earth. Thou hast been trampled on by every passer-by. Thy haughty invaders have disdained to call thee a nation. They have wished to sweep thee, with thy language and thy institutions and thy religion, from the face of the earth. Yet, lo! that which men despised and rejected, the same has become the corner-stone of the edifice of God. The more they trampled on thee, the more deeply didst thou cast thy roots; the more they shook thy aged trunk, the more rapidly didst thou shoot forth thy far-spreading branches.

What is there in nature more beautiful to behold than a majestic forest tree in the spring-time, as it decks itself with the luxuriance of its foliage and blushes in the pride of its variegated blossoms? How you wish it could remain ever thus undisturbed! But that ought not to be; for then it would live and die in selfish barrenness. To be of immortal usefulness it must, first, be shorn of its beauty; the fierce equinoctial blasts must wrench its seeds from it, and spread them broadcast over the earth, and cover them from the wrath of winter with the leaves torn from its moaning branches. Thieving birds must carry away its fruits to scatter them on a distant soil. If, then, you return to view that noble plant after wind and storms have worked their will upon it, you will hardly recognize in the dreary, naked wood the object of your admiration a few months ago. But wait a little. The winter will soon be past, and

you will find that the harm has not been
serious, much less irreparable. It will bud
and blossom again in a glorious resurrec-
tion; and behold! far and near a thousand
saplings are springing up, each reproducing
the vigor of the parent stock. In like
manner, whilst nations which have enjoyed
serene prosperity have, so far as the sacred
cause of Revelation is concerned, lived and
died sluggish and inactive, Ireland, rudely
shaken by every wind of heaven, has, without losing much at home, multiplied herself in every quarter of the globe. Why,
then, ought we not to bless the whirlwind
which has scattered our noble race? The
tears of the exile were necessary to the
propagation of the faith; and whilst we
sympathize sincerely with the suffering
individuals, we must never lose sight of
the Divine purpose which their sufferings
are predestined to effect.

In the prosecution of this analogy between the life of St. Patrick and the history of his people, we discover another point of resemblance well worthy of consideration. St. Patrick was sent into captivity that he might become familiar with the language and customs of the people whom he was chosen to evangelize. So, too, the Irish, having been selected by the Lord for the important work of evangelizing a great part of the world, were subjected to the sway of that nation whose wonderful enterprise has made her language the most generally spoken by the human species. How little did the English dream, when they were planting their proud banner on every remote corner of the globe, on every island, on every coast, that Providence was making use of their ambition for the advantage of a nation which they despised and of a religion which they detested? Yet such the event proves to have been the case. England's discoveries and conquests simply paved the way for the Irish and their holy religion. England forced the Irish to drop the language of their fathers, and adopt that of their oppressors. She was but too glad to offer them her ships, and induce them to establish themselves in her colonies. But, my friends, England has lost, and is losing, her hold upon her colonial possessions; whereas the Irish and their blessed faith remain, and will remain, please God, till the end of time.

But let us bring this discourse to a conclusion. I have endeavored to show how far-reaching and enduring St. Patrick's work has been. He is become, in very deed, the father of a great nation, whose distinctive trait is its inviolable fidelity to God. Like their apostle, the Irish people were great and holy in the days of their prosperity; their greatness and holiness were enhanced during the long ages of their trials; and they have arrived at the summit of spiritual glory now that God has scattered them far and wide to be the salt of the earth and the light of the world.

Be mindful, therefore, of your mission, Irishmen and children of Irishmen, and at the same time appreciate the formidable responsibility which that mission lays upon you. No doubt, our great race will achieve its sublime destiny, notwithstanding the frailties of individuals; for though there may be weak and unworthy brethren amongst us—though there may be Irishmen who are drunkards, and Irishmen who are dishonest, and Irishmen who by other vices dishonor their country and scandalize the unbeliever—yet the mass of our people are, in practice and principle, "true to the faith." But it is well for us to remember that it was for no trivial purpose we or our fathers were transplanted into this fertile region. Divine Providence has placed us here, as on a mountain top, that men may have full scope to observe us, and may value our faith by the works of righteousness which it engenders within us. And, my friends, this great American nation into which we are incorporated deserves well of us; for when the old world had cast us off, it received us with open arms and welcomed us to an equal share in the blessings which the Lord of nature lavishes upon it. But it is our privilege, as well as our duty, to make a grateful return for this hospitable reception; for whilst America possesses in abundance gold and silver, food and raiment, yet, in a higher sense, she is sadly destitute. She lacks that better food which fills the soul, and this food she must receive from our hands. Faith perfected almost to vision, supernatural love of God, unsullied chastity—these are the spiritual riches with which the half-clad, half-starved emigrant comes laden to these shores, and they are an ample remunera-

tion for the many kindnesses which he re-
ceives.

In conclusion, let us, as is meet and
proper, cease not to offer up fervent prayers
to God, through the intercession of St.
Patrick, for the welfare of the land of our
fathers. She has suffered enough; she
has been tried enough. "How long, O
Lord, how long!" Already through the
many rents made by the stormy indigna-
tion of the civilized world in the wretched
patchwork of this last of Irish Coercion
Acts which is now weighing heavily upon
her, we can catch most certain glimpses of
those happier days, long sighed for, long
deferred; and I am confident that when
the noon-day of her temporal glory shall
arrive, Ireland will remain, as she has hitherto remained, true to her mission, "true
to the faith." But of this I am sure, that
if, as we earnestly desire, peace with its
abundance and liberty with her manifold

blessings return to nestle among her green hills, she will ever look back with an honest pride upon the ages of her sorrows; she will "rejoice for the days in which she was humbled, for the days when her eyes saw evils."